What Rainbows Reveal

What Rainbows Reveal

Liturgies of Resilience

James Jennings Jr.

The Book Clearing Press LLC
New York

What Rainbows Reveal

The Book Clearing Press LLC
54 STATE STREET, STE 804 #10295
ALBANY, NY 12207
www.thebookclearingpress.com
Contact via email: info@thebookclearingpress.com
Reclaiming Resilience Through Restorative Reading

First Printing: October 2023
ISBN:979-8-218-30357-0

Printed in the United States of America

<u>Dedication</u>

To My Mother, Joyce
(and some things you've learned me)

You did really well

Sometimes I wonder how you did/do it
But in my confusion I remember:
You're a reminder of the magic of faith
"Faith is reserved for the future"
Saul Williams once said that
I'd like to add determination to that as well
For real Vulnerability, Growth, and Trust
require the fullness of our presence to be present.

So I have faith that we can make this human experience
more equitably just, as you taught me.

To equip my heart and mind
with the tactics of Courage and tools of Love,
To realign and redefine our redefining ways when we speak
of Integrity and Human Responsibility,
This is more than the haves and have-nots
For why are we here if not to craft stories
and listen to them
 after all, we can all do that.

Just look at Janet, your Godchildren,
your students, and the coworkers you organize

Yes, you did a very very good job, thank you.

Well, I wish I could be like a bird in the sky
How sweet it would be if I found I could fly
Oh, I'd soar to the sun and look down at the sea
And then I'd sing 'cause I'd know
How it feels to be free Lord, Lord, Lord, yeah!

"I Wish I Knew How It Would Feel To Be Free"
Nina Simone, Billy Taylor & Dick Dallas

Blackbird singing in the dead of night
Take these broken wings and learn to fly
All your life
You were only waiting for this moment to arise

"Blackbird"
Paul McCartney, The Beatles

CONTENTS

You <u>are</u> Inspiration

Liturgy

1: a eucharistic rite

2: a rite or body of rites prescribed for public worship

3: **<u>a customary repertoire of ideas, phrases, or observances</u>**

I
LITURGIES OF BREATH

What IF we could **place**

Our hand over heart
Direct our breath
To the center of the palm

What IF we could **chant:**

Love, Courage, Peace, Justice
Peace, Love, Courage, Justice
Courage, Peace, Love, Justice

What IF we could **commit**

To Redefinition
Reexamination
To design the redesign
To embark its dissolution

To Begin Anew

A(new)

If the day can begin
and then start anew,
As time drifts and swims
amidst New York and New Zealand,
Then the same goes for you
For whatever stage you're in.

You may recognize your fear
But promise me you won't give in
And tell yourself
I'm far too old
To fail and try again

Eternal Resonances

We are mortal

But what we (can) create

Lasts eternity

Therefore we are co-conspirators

and co-creators of reality.

We define and make rules

Some say "to rule"

And we are ruled

Don't like it

But we convince each other we need it.

How long must we go on agitating our conscience

re-scribing the language we inhabit

when we know right from wrong,

As we easily discern right from left

Up from down.

Love never wears the mask of enclosure
Love breathes, gathers, then welcomes
Always.

We have the capacity to create
eternal resonances of goodwill and love
We really really do.

Zephyrs of Change

Let my eyes not water

At the sight of turbulent doubts

Clouding within your eyes;

forming in the corners of your mind

Whose tongue convinced your soul

of its interminable wandering?

Don't you know the sun envies you;

Your smile invokes heaven's thundering.

Let not trepidation halt your journey

Let not your heart don the wickedness you receive.

But with every vibrating pulsation:

Sense the Sorrow

        Perceive the Pain

                Heal the Hurt

Of your transgressors.

        Of yourself.

                For your future Self

Be a bully for justice,

an advocate for transformative peace

For as we now know,

changes in the wind can be felt

but only seen,

when the zephyrs of the sky forbid the breeze's frailty.

Fresh.Start

You need:

A fresh start

since your mental's spoiled and soon-to-be-rotten

You tell yourself to tighten up

But the thing you've forgotten:

Paradise is not a place

Heaven's not some holy space,

Configure Bliss

Consider this can exist within your gaze

In the recesses of your brain

Ingrained

Tucked beneath those mental chains

Evade the notion to tame "who you *is*"

And celebrate who you became

How you overcame

Day after Day

In every growing stage

Despite what others had to say

Somehow you made a way.

freedom is

Like that certain sense;
freedom
is
When you let the microwave ring at night
when everyone is sleeping,

—Of being heard—

Sucking the mango seed clean as you please
when everyone is looking
Dancing in the shower
when you're already running late.

If our conception of freedom is based on a premise of
continual death — a common excuse for
exorbitant military expenditures and war —
then we have grossly undermined our creative capacity
to imagine <u>life devoid of violence and domination</u>.

art is

Salvation (at the end of a song)

Deliverance (at the close of a dance)

Liberation (with the lifting of a pen)

Freedom (like the unfurling of film)

As a penultimate line jettisons expectation

We get what we get

But always, we get what we give

That <u>capture of self-release</u>

Is what art truly is to me

God is

Because God is (and will always be)
that which you make them
— yes, even after doctrinal beliefs—
God must still attend to *your* capacities
to negotiate their placement in *your* life
That is, if you choose (them).

God is dead to those dead to God
God is alive to those enlivened by God

Who is God?
Whose is God?

That is for you to investigate.

Don't Worry

There are a lot of things I want you to do
Worry, is not one of those things.
If anything, worry that in worrying
you anticipate a *justified* recurrence
of loss, hurt, and harm.

They say learn to laugh at your failures
Setbacks happen
But your presence need not digest
the lack you feel within

Jimmy B. told us to vomit up those inner lies
The ones Ellison warned us originate
from their wicked "inner eyes"
So what can *you* do?

My mother told me to sing
My grandmother: read
My sister taught me rest
I tell myself to breathe.

Devised To Be

when we decide to make work our living:

We decide to live by work

Work determines why we live

And because we have decided

Are Devised

To

Live by work

And not by love,

We fail to honor the value of human life

To really seeeeeeeeeeeeeeeeeeeeeeee

each other.

!

Walk and

live your

life as if

an

!

erects

your

spine!

The Sanctity of Breath

Can we pause when needed
and let Breath recollect
as a choir anticipates a rest?

Can I wonder how the waters speak unto me
as I wander here with you
just to worry, then forget
how my sweat stirs your breath
"Maybe you should rest," you say to me.
you: meaning we
as we ponder why on earth
the birds and beasts haven't terminated us yet.

We deserve each other's time
If only we acted as we could...

I now understand the sanctity of breath
Protect your tempo and reset.

You & Me Against "fear"

Think of a fear.

The one that shivers your mind…

The one you never speak aloud…

GRAB IT!

now silently scream at it (disrespectfully, trust me):

"I *will* conquer you!!!"

Your Fear:

"Good."

"If by faith you can believe,

By faith you will succeed. Good…Good."

***

Fear and Faith share sides of a coin.

Fearing personal triumph over one's fear

leaves one doubly frightful.

And one must live.

Practicing Certainty

100% of the time when you thought

something was in your shoe

You checked

(On yourself)

And your answer was found

With your mind and soul

Let yourself know

you are certainly able to check on them too.

And...

I'm excited for you.

We are Better Softer

We are better when we are softer
We're at our best in our most tender moments
(and we know it too!)
The riddle of life it may be...

Ijustwishwecouldseebiggerthancolorbiggerthansexth
anclassareyouseriouslyseriousiswhatifeelcursethedesi
reforgreedanddominationwecalleachotherfriendandf
ueltheliethelietthatwearenotalikethisischildrensmatte
rsletusgrowtheabsolutef*ckupifnottomorrowhowabo
utinaweekIgiveusthattimetotransformevencaterpilla
rscraverenewal

We Wondered Why

We wondered why Wendy worriedly

worked late on Wednesdays

Or why she wept when the whirling winds

whistled at night.

We did not understand why

she wandered West in winter

Or waded in the water before the sun's early wake.

We just wish she were here

Still here.

More Than What You Know

You are more than what you know

You are more than what you do

You are more

You'll be more

You'll become more than that you fear

Kaedama

"Just one more bowl!"

I can't remember a time when I didn't order Kaedama

don't count that one date when I forced myself cute!

Irrespective of this reprehensible act of self-defiance,

me and ramen, we got a thing going on.

Maybe, unlike my 3 lifetime crushes,

it never feared my pursuance

It acknowledged my resolution to be filled

and in the midst of company,

over lessons of chopstick etiquette

and suitable toppings,

we listened to learn and learned to listen.

It was like when Miles delighted in Bird,

it made 'em *sorta* Dizzy

One said, "I'll take a swig of your fifth, but I'll take mine

flat — preference of taste."

And also when Trane listened to Miles,
then Miles listened to Trane.

"You likin' to change *too* much."
"Well, you got ears."

Community in Growth

We must strive to be individuals
and respect our Human access to eternal individuality.
In this way, we will extend the grace and empathy others
rightfully deserve
And we can accept (not tolerate)
difference(s)
as constant community in growth

Allabout Joy!

Why must my fears score horror films just for my ears

And turn my hard stone bones to a thin sheer veneer;

If only I could hear

how sunny skies protect their cheer.

Lying low beneath the sun

Growing to glow and whereupon,

A gentle breeze now whispers to me:

"Confront yourself, my son

Embrace *all* that you've become."

Constant comparison silences glee

I consider and I think:

Who and what is controlling me?

Truly, who, am I trying to be?

Breathe

And then I remember:

As the skies storm, rage, then clear,

I too, must be willing to earn and learn

Joy while I'm here

2
LITURGIES OF
FORGIVENESS

I'm learning to forgive myself and others.

But it's extremely difficult because in some way

you have to respect yourself enough to know

you'll give it a better shot next time;

to not cave into complacency when

distance becomes desirous,

and Lord knows I'm comfortably dispirited.

How is it that change accompanies chosen growing pains?

I need me here for me when no one's listening

I need me to learn pride is draining my life

I need me to tell me it's going to be okay

I need me to hear me to forgive me

and I need me to be honest.

Breakthrough

Breakdown

To

Breakthrough

Somehow,

The scalding hot shower fails to cleanse,

And the bath water blistering my shins refuses to boil

the guilt from within.

...

But behind it all,

Underneath it all;

When I can pull myself into *that* Room

—That air of Truth I tentatively breathe as if allergic—

Is me

As me

If only I'll allow myself to peer within.

Your Shine

Don't even dare disrespect your dignity
or attempt to diminish your shine

Why do that?

The Disrespected Self

Heartbreaks and failures are hard
But what was harder to navigate was the internal shame
that my Self disrespected its own capacity
to be resilient
I was shunning me for doubting my ability
to succeed
And that was the hardest reality to release.

The Hardest Thing To Do

If the hardest thing to do

Is *self*-reflect

Then what does that make of

self-acceptance?

Roosted

Birds aren't concerned with the speed of the jet

Or that it can fly,

They are capable as they are,

After all, they're still high in the sky.

YouCare

Count the stretch marks and newly formed grey hairs

Don't be afraid to admit that you care,

Acknowledge failures and shortcomings

Humanize yourself, there's no need to keep running.

Black Tiger Lily

sometimes my girl tears I'm too lonely

But I assure her I'm fine,

Add a "really" for deceptive emphasis.

And here is partly why:

A "friend" or what we disguise it to be

Is too fickle and frivolous

for the types of humans we are meant to be.

Let's look for partners and extended family members

Let's look to change, adapt, and learn

Aja's mother doesn't know they are sisters

and I think my father fails the same.

Let's befriend the notion of indeterminacy

For do we "really" know?

have it all figured out?

All we *can* do is feel.

Then we "think" to justify "real"

I   think too much

is

my crime

For

the body

I enshrine

In this place

I

better

(GET)

Jiggy!

But I assure her that I'm fine
For real, like a black tiger lily.

...how are we fine?

Strange.Heart

Don't be a stranger to your own heart...

Do you know every avenue and road
in the town you call home?
Can you rattle off with haste
every alley, street, and highway?

Does your heart know you're home
when you've left it all alone?

Need I set its safety alarm,
to disarm wanton charm;
you only respond to unwanted harm.
Yet your heart remains worn like yarn

Lest your heart be equipped with GPS
Your lifelong mission involves continually finding it

A Dialogue with God:

"The First shall be last and the last shall be first"

With the atrocities they *continually* commit
should they even be in line?
Surely their doctrine and actions do not align
Saints, we fail to be
but at least we can honestly say we're trying!

We exclaim, "I love you Lord, You heard my Cry!"
And though faith is stronger than sight,
I question: Have you truly heard *our* plight?
Have our wails been hushed in the silence of the night?
Or our suffering, justified through biblical text
which persuades them they're right?

"Break the shackles off my feet so I can dance"

How can I praise you in my wretched circumstance?
Revenge we want not, though tempting

We shall persists and advance
over old transmogrified chains
We were never given an equal chance.

Twice, now thrice have I forgiven their ways Lord,
Enact your justice as you promised,
We're losing hope and that we cannot afford.

3
LITURGIES OF RELEASE

Dear Reader,

In this section you will hear me cry,

question, argue, and ultimately struggle.

I want you to know that while hope remains

a functional and necessary framework

to inspire contemporary liberation movements

(movements that honor our daily experience and existence

in their belief, rehearsal, and insistence on improving global

living conditions and thereby upholding the dignity, beauty,

and inherent complexity life requires us to respect...)

[release]

I still question, often antagonistically,

the notion that "We Are Family"

or "All You Need Is Love"

or even the anthemic chorus that "We Gon' Be Alright."

Working through these questions,

I present to you a collection of offerings I can best describe

as emotionally incisive and politically grounding;

to convey the inner stirrings of my soul and mind.

A Great Cry

What can you do when your eyes beg for release?

When the only thing fighting back tears is

the biting of tongue or the newfound desire

to look upwards.

When now you cherish the restroom stall, sometimes

the grime of it all pales to the safe haven of privacy.

I need a good cry.   We need a great cry.

The kind that chuckles into a laugh

as you stumble to dry the aftermath.

What a beautiful rage it is to accept

Some goodbyes age the soul temporarily

We call it *weight* — "that was heavy, man"

"*...release, my love, release into peace*"

And I promise...

The heart will withstand the labor grief demands

And through it all

your capacity to love will only expand.

Changed & Unchained

"Teardrops clear the haze of my heart"

And in some way,

You and I want to be heard

Need to be seen

Sacrificing breath as we gaze

...

Do my actions look like Love?

Does it feel *like* Love?

Do the words I say

do they sound like

like Love ought to sound?

Do my actions look like Love?

"My deepest God is Me"

Reflected in the mirror

And in the stillness of water

That makes even more profound

the image: it's the God *in* me

Raise changed and unchained

God is in you too!

A Lesson and a Blessing

If I try, I fail.

But if I fail to try, I've already been defeated

Even when my talents are exceeded,

The lessons from failure won't be repeated.

Struggle legitimizes strength,

Don't let your confidence be depleted.

Either Way

Who's really in control:

The caller or the receiver

The owner or the retriever

The truth sayer or deceiver

The agnostic or believer

The dispassionate or the overachiever

Your anger or your ego

Are you so eager to announce victory

over subscription that you choose neither?

Either way, all follow procedure

Expectantly...

Reluctantly...

"You can only be a dreamer for so long, simply fall in line"

Dear ego, I think I will decline

and restrain the yearning to resign

Defeat should not be viewed as a failure or a crime

After all, you have to get up

if you're determined to climb!

Rain In Me

Rain keeps following us,

Look up to see the Sky foam.

Drowsy, still waking

As platinum peridots punctuate his wake.

Breathing, then smiling, expelling Sun

warming all under her embrace

She, scooping down, turns to highlight my "bad side"

Reminding me:

That which I hide

sooner or later will surface and rise

to the point where neither charm nor guile

can quell what's destined for the Light.

Rain follows me

Though I cannot tell you why

I may philosophize or surmise

I may choose to cry or whine

But whatever I *decide*,

I'll recognize my life is still mine.

Different.Directions

your changes will sustain you,
after all, you are evolving.
use them as chances to propel you
towards a direction;
though not always forward.

going straight may seem to equate
with clear-cut actions in your brain,
but I'd implore you to explore
destinations you'd otherwise ignore.

Mining My Purpose

I wish to discern the determination to mine
my purpose out the depths of duplicitous doubt
To safeguard the sanctuaries of sacrifice
evident in, around, and about me.

I wish to articulate
—gently and convincingly—
that though doubt rests here,
he is not of my own *true* creation;
That my Being, as it be
Is and will surmount
And shall surpass
And shall outshine!

Dare To Say No

Race,Gender, Class.........

A societal group project:

perennially unfinished

uncared for

incomplete

Group members fail to communicate or cooperate

Some take more responsibility

others none

All suffer

Still they do not care...

Still *we* make a way.

Good White Boys

What traverses the minds of those "good white boys"

when one of their brethren kills one of my brethren,

as one indolently arrests a gnat as it

climbs fearlessly to new heights?

And I mean the *good* white lads

Ones to whom even I am convinced and disarmed

by their well-meaning nature and disposition

When will reserved fury exact yet another tragedy?

No one held accountable...the script repeats;

itself nauseated by the fecund terror...

...of lawlessness and loss, of never-changing sames with

grinning pastors, restless organists, and overplayed

hymns with mortuary expenses and chicken & mac and

cheese brought over to line stomachs and nourish souls,

where sung alibis of witness soar miraculously —

but *if* it is so well then why doesn't my soul *feel* that way;

forgetting now what our last conversation was about

and what they told me to always remember over the
phone last time, if only I had come home in time and...

And still I wonder what traverses the hearts of those
"honest guys" who *demand* my forgiveness,
expect my understanding and whose flesh is armored
by the death of my own destiny.

For I'd like to think
I can have white friends, male that is
Yet in this act of trying, am I but hewing out
a forged dignity, recognition of Self,
position in the Family?
I do not know...

Seizure

Over-exposed Light
Flat Rubber Tire
Bustling Boulevard

Orange, yellow + reds
dot the road that lies ahead
urging me to stop.

Unaware of the internalized cop
Who'd do anything to avoid being shot
or resuscitated on a medical cot
Who'd risk nothing to justify Daddy's safety talks
Questioning the hour, glancing down at his watch
Stammering to seize the only threat he could govern:
His breath was offense enough;
for this arrest would beget his death.

Spikes in the Shower

I was never the spikes-in-the-shower

kind of baseball player

But my right knee would tell you

it was always in constant danger.

The Hot Corner, as they call it

attracted lasers disguised in leather

and battered me around like 2-0 count

I can say I was a stranger to constant failure & defeat

Not in life, just baseball.

But on second review,

I know why my teeth weren't chipped

on the shower floor after practice;

The payoff was too great

I was a snitch: non-loyalty for non-allies

I knew then what bullies could do

Why give them grace when they deplore

you and all that you seek to do?

For Gain or Protection

Part of what it means to grow up in America

—philosophically, socially, and culturally—

is *to become* racist-in-thought and *to become* obsessed

or well informed with the tenets of

settler colonialism & white supremacy

for gain or for protection.

This is not love

This is not life.

Foolish

For Emmet, Trayvon, Sandra,

etc...

They laughed when I told them my biggest fear

was a white woman.

That when I see one on the street,

my heartbeat quickens a little

My glands begin to perspire — I get on edge.

They called me foolish when I told them:

When walking in the same direction,

I always stay in front

Hoodie down

Pants up.

That's what they told me would keep me alive

I listened

And so I'm still here

For this is not *my* world, as you can see

I am living by *their* rules

Guided by fear

Disillusioned by hope

Directed by my parents who

rehearsed these patterns into me

We know not another way — to survive

Those that thrive still struggle with it daily

They hide from the truth:

comportment didn't make them whiter

They believed in lies, though mostly self-contrived,

They spoke of boot-straps, cold sweat, and dreams forlorn

Reminding us we could have made it if we had just tried...

All of these thoughts ran through my mind

Standing over their open caskets.

I wished to God they wouldn't have laughed,

perhaps maybe they'd still be alive.

Humanity First

A political party

Should not be justification for backwards thinking

or crimes against humanity,

you still have to be a good person.

I don't care what your ideology tells you to believe

You must put humanity first.

I Knew The Kids Were Right!

When the glitter of life starts to fade...

Scream within: "I knew the kids were right!"

....

It's no wonder they made god *he*.

Sentiment to him pales

To Mother.

We *know* our mothers.

If god, the giver of life,

Was *made* she

My Lord — their shame

Under motherly gaze

Would choke the life out of them.

Therefore,

Do not take what they preach

to be the Truth for you.

Tenderness is virtue, so just do you.

When the glitter of life begins to dissipate,

Coal mine the joy of children's laughter from within.

A Newfound Home

What if our tears had names
labeled with emotions we could not claim,
My troubled soul would weep for joy
A feeling I've yet to ascertain.

And what if our tears had eyes
that'd cry when we smiled,
My happy tears would roll
onto your shoulder; a newfound home.

4
LITURGIES OF CREATION

We're all Artworks in progress,

Some Masterpieces take longer

to finish than others

Give it time.

Give yourself the gift of compassionate patience.

In the process, never dim your Inner Shine

We are Designers of our Destiny

So, let's Create Anew!

Love Crusades

[set in someone's university religion class]

We could come up with ritualized customs

and practices of Love

Like religion itself is a "practice"

We could *virtue-name* religious denominations:

"We're *GreatestLove!*"   "Join us, we're *Lovegrace!*"

"First Luv!"

"Don't hesitate to stop by, we are *Luv Reigns Forever!*"

"Welcome to *Lots of Love!*"

Of course, one may say,

"Well aren't those the same thing?"

No, ours won't be based on a father, son, and ghost.

But instead, your grandma, your child, my uncle

And we will wage Love Wars

Love Crusades

To actualize sisterly concern with brotherly handshakes

We *should* make this Love we have

evidently evident to see, feel, taste, hear, and sense.

"Christianers"

A Teach(er)

A Gamble(r)

Verb become Noun

Must practice what they claim to be

Not the same for religion

Believers should *do*

But they don't *have* to

Religion is a thing

Religionism: a practice

untangle the two

become "Christianers"

And check back into *this* world.

Why I Sing

Sometimes I sing
To suggest that I am free
You wouldn't think otherwise
Given such fanciful melodies

Sometimes my lips evolve into a flute
I'm a songbird refusing to be mute

To tell you the truth, during my youth
The first concert stage I knew
belonged in the living room underneath my roof

....

Today I'm finding happiness within voice cracks
It lets me know that I am trying

I'm locating jubilation in the quiver of my tone
Know these shedding tears have shown amidst this
performance not entirely my own

I'm discovering delight within early entrances
Simply enthusiasm evading composure

And botched grace notes are slowly becoming my friend
They're just colorful notes bent blue; let's call 'em jazz!

The New Day

Life is but a movie
A superhero one at that!
Some aimlessly roam around
never realizing their potential power,
While others never settle down,
they're too busy dabbling around;
never realizing that talents
aren't the same as destined callings.

"I think you are a healer"
"And you may be a teacher"
"And you have your way with words,
You just might be a great speaker!"

I'm saying you ease the pain,
While you plant seeds of wisdom in my brain,
And you always know what to do
and what to say
Without hesitation, strain, or blame.

Use your life to tell a story

Live your life, leave us a lesson

For as a collective we will use our gifts

to revive the New Day.

B(u)y You

Down a frosted glass brick broadway

Running through alley to avenue to highway

Hear them singing hymns

Of love and sacrifice:

"Call me when you get off from work!"

-hooooooonk!-

"You're going to miss your bus Junior,

I've seen you move faster for that ice cream truck.

Come on!"

Human

Care

And because someone has to feed the blackbird

someone has to oil the altar

A recursive loop unto itself:

You are.

Are you?

You do.

Do you?

Be you

You better be good to your ~~effing~~ Self

I hope you feel my urgency

For I need you to thrive, not simply survive

So...

Be kind

b(u)y you

first.

What Rainbows Reveal

What *do* rainbows reveal?

Resilience matters

Optimism is struggle

Your yesterday is not today

Gratitude inspires growth

Boundless bravery reaches and teaches

Integrity is measured in action

Vivacity for the ultimate justice of things

How do I know?

Because *Rainbow* only shows its face

After *Rain* has finished its stay.

Renewal after pain

That which *they* hate

They'd actually *love* to love;

For they do 'overstand' our plight.

But blood stains their hands

and guilt sullies their sight

and fear, like a looking glass,

reflects that which immobilizes *just* consciousness:

To listen

To connect

To expand

To change

****

I asked the tiny old gnome:

"Dear Leprechaun Sir,

Just where is *my* share of gold?"

Smugly sneering he peers through me,

"It appears yours isn't to take.

Come along next year m'boy,

you'll simply have to wait!"

"Wait!?," he thought.

Why exactly would he wait?

"For???"

The elf fixed its features

transforming before his eyes into a pixie,

brilliant and bright like a fresh coat of snow.

"I was wondering why you...I mean the leprechaun-guy

before...told me I had to wait?"

"Could you not understand?!" She shrieked.

"The rainbow's gold, you see, must be hoar—,

must be *protected* at all costs to ensure

everyone's share in the lot.

Please don't be upset, your *kind* can't touch this yet!"

"Mhmm, everyone...my kind huh..."

He noticed the gold, pretty as it was,

began to sweat under the sun's torrid glare.

Before he could speak, his soul whispered within:

"No need to wait, my son.

What they got, you may not have.

But what they *need*, well,

they may never earn or learn that."

He slowly strolled away,

In his head, a dance tune started to play.

He shuffled his feet,

Now skipping to the beat

He hummed along and whistled the song

and finally bellowed a most glorious tone!

His gold was never achieved, but he remembered:

how diamonds adorned his speech,

his teeth and cheeks.

And they radiated abundantly

all throughout his community.

What a joyous witness to behold!

A Rainbow's Revelation:

To change *is* to be

You are...

I am...

We are Beautified

Limitless Reach

Does the sun need a reminder to know she is bright?

Does the moon and do the stars need permission

to cast their light at night?

Does the ocean need a notice to know he is deep?

And does the sky ever question its limitless reach?

No.

And neither should you.

THANK YOU FOR READING!

James J.

Scan Me!